LOCAL HABITATS

THE
LIVING
HOUSE

Nigel Hester

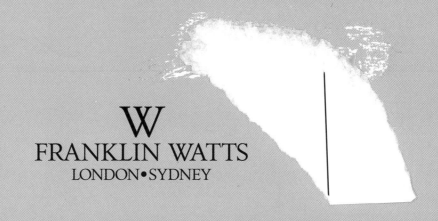

W
FRANKLIN WATTS
LONDON•SYDNEY

This edition 2004

Franklin Watts
96 Leonard Street
London EC2A 4XD

Franklin Watts Australia
45-51 Huntley Street
Alexandria
NSW 2015

Copyright © 1991

First published as Nature Watch: The Living House
Editor: Su Swallow
Designer: K and Co
Illustrations: Angela Owen, Ron Haywood
Phototypeset by Lineage Ltd, Watford

Photographs: Heather Angel 7tr, 8t, 8br, 9bl, 9br, 11tl, 17 (inset), 20t,
22bl, 22br, 27br, 28c; Ardea 12bl, 12 (centre inset), 14t, 17tr, 24bl,
28bl, 29cr; Biofotos/ Paul Ormond 15; Bruce Coleman Ltd 17tl; Nigel
Hester 4 (all), 5 (all), 7, 7bl, 10 (top inset), 10 br, 11tr, 18c, 18b, 20bl,
20bc, 20br, 23tl, 23tr; Eric and David Hosking 7br, 8bl, 10t, 10bl,
11bl, 11br, 12t, 13t, 14b, 19 (both), 21 bl, 21br, 25, 27t, 28t, 29t; David
Hosking/Ian Rose 29br; Frank Lane Picture Agency 9t, 13c, 13b, 15tl,
15bl, 18t, 22t, 24t, 24br, 27bl, 29cl; Oxford Scientific Films 12br;
Survival Anglia 28br; Barrie Watts 29bl.

Front Cover: Chris Fairclough Colour Library (main picture), Eric and
David Hosking (inset right), Frank Lane Picture Agency (inset left).

A CIP catalogue record for this book is available from the British Library

ISBN: 0 7496 5657 3

Printed in Belgium

CONTENTS

HOUSES AND GARDENS

What kind of house do you live in? Do you have a garden? This book tells you about some of the animals, large and small, that you might find in and around your house. Some of them will spend most of their lives indoors. Others will come in from the garden from time to time to find food and shelter. You can also read about some of the wild plants that might appear in your garden.

The variety of wildlife that is attracted to share your home will depend on what kind of house you live in and on how old the garden is.

Few creatures live in new houses *(above)*. The cottage *(left)* will be visited by animals from the nearby countryside. In towns, street lamps *(below)* attract night-flying insects.

An old garden *(left)*, especially one with a shed, contains more wildlife than a new garden *(below)*. Pet cats *(above)* and dogs may chase small mammals and insects.

More wildlife can be found in old houses than in new ones. Wooden timbers, old stone walls, cellars and attics are some of the places that will eventually be invaded by animals from outside. When a new house is built, it takes a few years for animals to move in, although some tiny creatures may live in or on the building materials.

Gardens attract insects, birds, mammals and wild plants. An old garden has more wildlife than a new one. A new garden will only have creatures living in the soil and in the grass. As plants, shrubs and trees grow up, they provide food and shelter for a wide variety of animals.

INDOORS AND OUT

When animals move into houses the conditions they meet are often quite different from those outside. In the garden, rain provides water for drinking. Most places indoors are very dry. There is more daylight outside, too. In the house, animals run a much bigger risk of being disturbed by people than they do in the garden. Some animals find it difficult to survive for long in such conditions, but others have adapted very well to life indoors.

Some animals, such as carpet beetles and clothes moths, have become so well adapted that they do not need water at all. Other animals are nocturnal, moving about at night when most people are asleep.

The main advantages of living indoors for wild animals are shelter, warmth in winter, and food – particularly in the kitchen. The outside of a house also supports a number of animals, from wasps and spiders to nesting birds. Some plants live on the outside, too, taking root in holes in the walls and roof.

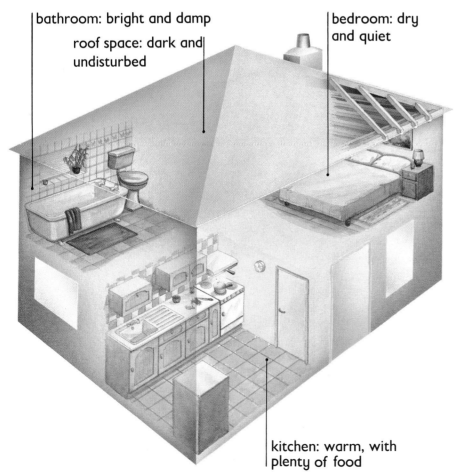

bathroom: bright and damp

roof space: dark and undisturbed

bedroom: dry and quiet

kitchen: warm, with plenty of food

◁ A house offers many different types of habitat. Some animals that move in are not fussy about where they stay, while others are usually found in one particular kind of place.

Lichens and mosses might grow on the roof tiles or slates of older houses (opposite, main picture). House martins (bottom right) or swallows might nest under the eaves. Snails (top right), spiders and some insects may be found on walls. At night, moths and insects may fly in through an open window, attracted by the light. Some tiny creatures spend the winter asleep in the corners of windows.

LIFE IN THE KITCHEN

The kitchen is probably the favourite place in any house for animals. It is usually warm and light, and steam from cooking provides moisture as it condenses back to water on the window and other cold surfaces. Scraps of food on the table and floor and in cupboards make an unending meal for many animals.

In the past, when kitchens were not very clean, many animals were pests. Today, although many animals go into kitchens, few are a serious threat to people's health. The housefly is an exception. It breeds on rubbish and animal dung, and carries bacteria that cause disease.

The lacewing *(above)* is a harmless house guest which may hibernate indoors. In the garden it feeds on aphids. The housefly *(below left)* is not so welcome. Cockroaches *(below)* are sometimes found in restaurant kitchens, where they feed at night.

Many small animals are associated with the food we eat. Biscuit beetles, meal moths (in grain) and flour mites are among the creatures found in stored food throughout the world. In the days of sailing ships, these creatures spread from country to country as they were carried in the food supplies for the voyage. Rats arrived in Britain over 250 years ago, stowed away on ships bringing grain from the Baltic countries.

The shiny body of the silverfish makes it easy to recognise. It likes damp places and feeds on food scraps, paper, glue and flour. The house mouse (below) eats food scraps, and even plaster, candle wax and wood. The brown rat (right) is found in grain stores and other outbuildings, and in old, dirty kitchens.

LIFE IN THE BATHROOM

The bathroom may seem a surprising place to find wildlife, but three things make it attractive to creatures. It is usually brightly lit, often warm and — after a bath or shower — there is plenty of moisture about.

On warm summer nights, a light left on in the bathroom will attract many insects. Moths, crane flies, lacewings and other night-flying insects may fly in through the window.

Spiders can be found in any room of the house, but the bathroom is one of the easiest places to see them. If they fall into the bath, for example, they cannot get out because their feet cannot grip the shiny surface.

Some algae and fungi grow in damp places indoors — on damp wallpaper, new plaster and damp wood, for example.

△ This buff ermine moth is resting on the bathroom window frame. The caterpillar of this moth *(top)*, which is very hairy, is common in gardens.

The small magpie moth *(below)* and the crane fly *(below left)* are also common in gardens, and may fly in through the open window.

Looking at moths

Moths are attracted to bright lights. When it is dark, hang a large white sheet on the washing line, or lay it on the grass. Shine the beam of a bright torch on to the sheet. Before long, moths will land on the sheet. Use an insect field guide to identify them, but do not touch them as they are very delicate.

△ The common house spider spins a sheet-like web to trap flying insects – especially houseflies.

◁ Dry rot fungus grows in damp wood in old houses, especially if they have been left empty.

▷ The cockchafer is one of the largest beetles found in Britain. On warm evenings in May it flies into houses. The larvae *(below)* live underground.

The bedroom makes a safe, quiet home for some animals. There is little food for scavenging insects, but most bedroom animals have become adapted to feeding on fabrics and carpets. The larvae (young forms) of clothes moths, house moths and carpet beetles devour clothes, curtains and carpets. Other insects feed on wood. The woodworm, or furniture beetle, is very common. If a piece of furniture infested with woodworm is brought into any room in the house, the beetle will gradually attack other wood in the building.

△ The white plume moth often lands on window panes at night. Its caterpillar feeds on hedge bindweed.

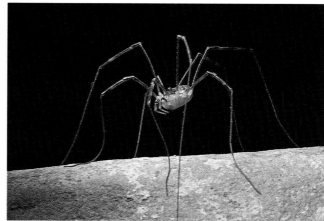

The furniture beetle *(below left)* lays eggs in timber. The larvae (woodworm) tunnel their way through the wood for up to five years. The adult beetles finally emerge out of holes in the wood *(far left)*.
▽ The harvestman likes dry places, so it may appear in the bedroom.

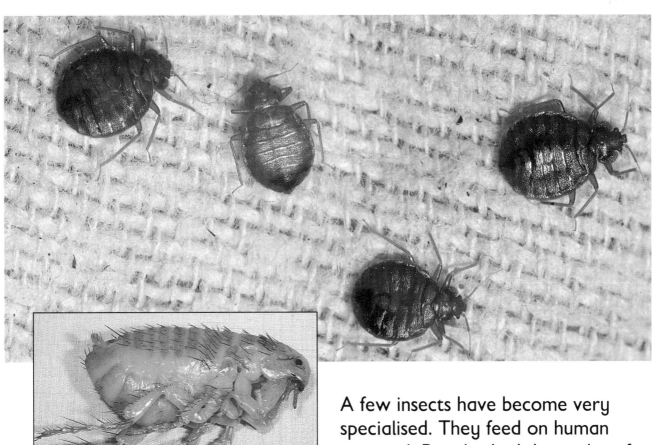

A few insects have become very specialised. They feed on human material. People shed dry scales of skin all the time. The scales drop off in bed on to the bedclothes. The house dust mite feeds on these scales. Unfortunately, the mite produces a fine dust that can affect people who suffer from asthma and hay fever.

The bed bug hides in the bed or under the skirting board during the day. At night, it attacks anyone sleeping in the bed.

Other creatures – bats, birds, mice, spiders, moths and mosquitoes, for example – may find their way into the bedroom, often by mistake, and startle people in bed.

△ The bed bug *(top)* bites people and sucks their blood, but it does not carry any disease. Cat fleas *(above)* may jump on to a person, but they cannot survive there.
▷ Earwigs are common in gardens. In winter they hibernate and some hide in the gap round the window frame.

LIFE IN THE ROOF

The roof houses a number of animals. Under the eaves, or edge of the roof, is a safe, sheltered spot for birds to nest. Other birds use the roof as a viewing platform to search for food. Birds that fly in large flocks may roost together at night on the roof. Some birds sing from the roof to attract a mate.

The loft space under the roof is warm, dark and quiet. Bats may rest in the loft during the day. The house sparrow, house mouse and insects such as bees and wasps may nest in it.

△ The serotine bat roosts and nests in or around the roof. It flies out at night to catch insects, especially beetles.

◁ Swallows build a nest of mud pellets under the roofs of houses and sheds.

▷ Starlings are very common in Britain. More than 4 million breed here. In the winter, a further 30 million birds migrate here from Europe. They fly in large flocks and roost on high buildings in towns and cities. They nest in tree holes, roof spaces and even in letter boxes, and are common visitors in the garden.

LIFE ON THE WALL

House and garden walls of stone and brick are home to a surprising number of plants and animals. With time, holes and cracks appear in walls exposed to the weather, and plant seeds lodge in these spaces. Once the plants become established, insects and other animals follow.

Mosses are among the first plants to appear on a wall, and in places where the air is clean, lichens are also quick to grow.

The main problem facing plants on walls is lack of moisture. Even when it rains, the water runs off the wall and away from the plant roots. The plants also have to be able to survive in direct, strong sunlight.

▽ The lichen shown here is one of the first signs of life on a new wall. It is common where the air is damp from heavy rainfall. The wall screw-moss forms dense tufts. It is quick to colonise new walls, but needs some cracks to grow in. The wall pennywort, with its tall spikes of flowers, grows on walls of stone or rock. It stores water in the base of its stem, which is pushed deep into cracks out of the sun. The sowthistle has waxy leaves to prevent it drying out in the sun.

Ivy may cover old walls completely, providing excellent cover for nesting birds. Some garden flowers, such as valerian and buddleia, may take root in old walls. Their flowers attract butterflies and other insects that feed on nectar.

All kinds of small creatures live or rest on walls *(below left)*. Some, like the wall brown butterfly and the jumping zebra spider, like to bask in the sun. Others look for damp, dark nooks and crannies. Snails graze on the algae.

zebra spider   millipedes   wall brown butterfly
woodlice   snails

wall pennywort   annual wall rocket
sowthistle   wall screw-moss

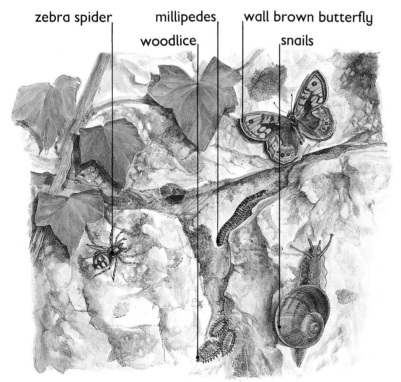

△ In summer, the mason bee lays its eggs in small holes in walls. Nectar and pollen are put in the hole for the grubs to feed on when they hatch.

The ruby-tailed wasp *(inset)* is a parasite. It lays its eggs inside the mason bee grubs. When the wasp grubs emerge, they feed on the bee grubs, killing them.

△ The wren often nests on ivy-covered walls. The vegetation hides the young birds.

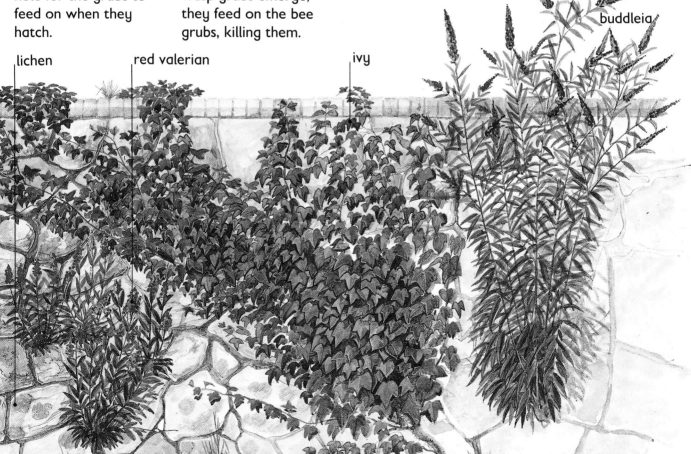

lichen

red valerian

ivy

buddleia

Garden sheds and other outbuildings provide shelter from heat and cold for many animals. They are able to roost, nest and hibernate in fairly peaceful surroundings.

Wasps and bees may spend the winter in the garden shed, and build their nest in the roof the following year. Spiders spin webs to catch the many insects that fly into the shed looking for shelter. Silverfish and other tiny creatures feed on old newspapers and cardboard that may be stored in the shed.

◁ Old sheds have large numbers of spiders, which spin masses of webs to trap both flying and ground insects.

△ Farm buildings attract all kinds of wild animals but old stone or wooden buildings are more suitable for some than the modern metal barns.

◁ The hornet *(far left)* sometimes makes its nest *(left)* in the roof of sheds or barns. Only a few eggs are laid in the papery nest, which hangs from the ceiling. The hornet is larger but more docile than the common wasp.

Large sheds and barns attract a wide range of wildlife, from tiny insects to large mammals. Mice, rats and other rodents are perfect prey for the barn owl, which likes to nest under the roof of old stone barns. Hedgehogs, bats and the edible dormouse may hibernate in sheds. Foxes make their dens beneath barns or sheds and rats dig nests and tunnels there.

△ Barn owls *(top)* have excellent eyesight and hearing. They hunt small mammals at night.

△ The edible dormouse *(above)* may raid apple stores in the shed or attic.

Tidy gardeners try to stop wild plants growing in their garden. They call the wild plants weeds. A weed is simply a plant growing where it is not wanted.

If wild plants are allowed to invade a garden, the first to arrive are annuals. An annual is a plant that grows to full size from seed in a year, and then dies. Dandelion is a common annual that quickly appears in the garden, growing from seeds blown on to the soil and warmed by the spring sunshine. Later in the year, perennials appear. These are plants that grow and flower for several years before they die. Perennials are tough plants with long taproots that can reach deep into the soil. Some are very difficult to get rid of once they establish themselves.

△ In the wild, horsetail grows in bogs and beside ponds and lakes. In the garden it grows in waterlogged ground.

◁ The germander speedwell spreads rapidly and often grows in lawns. It attracts flies, bees and other insects.

Bindweed *(below left)* is a climbing perennial which quickly smothers shrubs and hedges if it is not removed.
▽ Ribwort plantain is a perennial which often grows in lawns.

Making a wild flower garden

Why not set aside a small part of your garden for wild flowers? In the spring or summer, clear a bare patch of ground and see which plants grow first. To help you record the plants, you need a quadrat. Make a square frame from four pieces of wood 100cm long. Tie pieces of string across the frame to make 16 equal squares. Place the quadrat on your piece of ground and on squared paper make a note of the different plants growing in each square. If you do this at regular intervals through the year you will build up a picture of the plants colonising your wild garden.

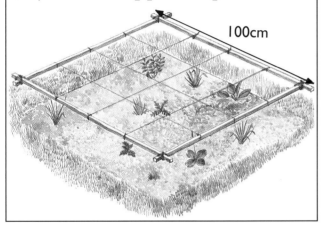

100cm

Some wild plants give us useful clues about the type of garden that we have. Docks and dandelions can grow in soil with few minerals in the top layer, because their long roots allow them to reach the minerals deep down. Plants such as horsetail and lady's smock only grow in damp soil, and so on.

Wild plants in a garden are not all a nuisance. Many of them attract insects and birds. It is a good idea to set aside a small area of the garden for wild flowers. If an area of grass is left to grow unchecked, wild flowers will appear there, too. The area has to be cut once or twice a year to prevent it becoming completely overgrown. By managing a patch of grass in this way it is possible to create a miniature hay meadow.

◁ Lady's smock is also called the cuckoo flower because it flowers when cuckoos return in spring. The caterpillar of the orange tip butterfly feeds on the leaves.

◁ Scarlet pimpernel flowers open in sunshine and close in cloudy weather. The plant grows in sandy and stony soil.

Different kinds of insects can be found at different times of year. Butterflies that have hibernated for the winter, such as the small tortoiseshell and the brimstone, can be seen flying on warm days even in February. Bees visit early spring flowers such as snowdrops and crocuses to gather nectar. As summer arrives, the number of insects reaches a peak. Masses of aphids attack garden plants. Flowers attract butterflies in the day and moths at night. In autumn, wasps eat fruit in the garden.

△ The nymphs (young stage) of frog hoppers produce white froth when they suck the sap from plants. The froth, known as cuckoo spit, protects the nymphs from predators, and stops them drying out in the sun.

When aphids are a nuisance in the garden, help is on hand from another insect. Ladybirds *(left)* can eat as many as 100 aphids a day. Their larvae *(below)* also eat aphids.

Large white butterfly

Small tortoiseshell butterfly

A garden full of butterflies

These are some of the flowers that will attract all kinds of butterflies to your garden. It is important to have a range of plants so that some are always in flower from early spring to late summer. It is also a good idea to grow plants such as nettles, thistles and dandelions, for caterpillars to feed on.

aubretia
(flowers in spring)

honesty (flowers in
early summer)

lavender
(flowers in summer)

buddleia
(flowers in summer)

ice plant
(flowers
in late summer)

Birds treat gardens rather like pieces of woodland. A mixture of open ground, flowers, shrubs and trees provides food, roosting places and nesting sites, just like a wood. A garden that is densely covered in trees is not very suitable for many birds, because they need space to spot predators, and room for flying.

Shrubs that produce berries are a valuable food source for many birds. Fruit trees are useful too. The crab apple tree often holds its fruit until winter, which provides a meal when other food is scarce. A patch of ground with wild flowers provides food for seed-eating birds. Thistles and teasels in particular encourage all kinds of finches to visit.

All birds need water to drink and to wash their feathers, so a pond will attract birds to the garden.

△ In the autumn, goldfinches are often seen in small groups, feeding on thistles and other tall weeds. The hedge sparrow, or dunnock *(below left)* eats insects and small seeds. The magpie *(right)* eats other birds' eggs. Blackbirds *(below)* feed on fallen fruit in autumn.

Feeding the birds

A good way to watch birds is to put food out for them in your garden. Only do this in winter, when their natural food is in short supply. Do not feed them in summer, because some food is harmful to the young chicks.

If you build a bird table, place it away from trees. Birds feel safer feeding in the open.

During the daytime, the garden is a busy place. Insects, birds and other small creatures are feeding, building nests or hunting. As night falls, these animals hide away to rest. But the garden is still full of life, even in the dark. Nocturnal animals, some of them quite large, emerge to find their food.

Mice, shrews and voles scurry about under the hedges and shrubs, hunting small animals and searching for seeds, berries and fruit. They are often in danger from owls flying over gardens in search of prey. Hedgehogs search for worms, slugs and beetles,

hedgehog

Perhaps the best time to see nightlife on your doorstep is just after rain, and on damp, misty evenings. Snails, slugs and earthworms will be out foraging for plant material. They in turn will attract hedgehogs, which feed on them.

On warm summer nights, look out for flying beetles. Use a torch to search the garden for nightlife. Frogs and toads will stay still if you shine a bright light on them.

fox

bat

moth

toad

rabbit

mouse

which are also active at night. Hedgehogs have poor eyesight, but have a keen sense of smell and hearing. The male can wander for about a mile each night. Moles dig tunnels at night in search of earthworms, but they also emerge to feed at the surface.

Rabbits visit country gardens at dusk and dawn, and may damage flowers and vegetables. Foxes are quite common even in town gardens. They often feed on rubbish.

Frogs and toads, and other animals that have to stay moist, come out of hiding at night.

△ The tawny owl hunts by night and roosts by day. It often visits parks and gardens with plenty of trees, in search of small mammals.

▽ Moles are not always welcome in gardens. As the mole digs underground, it throws up mounds of soil – mole hills *(below left)* – on the surface, which can spoil neat lawns.

Tracking snails
Snails come out at night to feed. To check on their movements day by day, place a small blob of paint on their shells. Search for them each day and plot their positions on a map of your garden. How far do they travel each night?

COMPOST HEAPS...

A compost heap is home to all kinds of wildlife. Fungi, worms, slugs and snails all help to break down the vegetation, which is put back on the soil to enrich it. The warmth inside the heap makes it a good nesting and hibernating place for some larger animals.

A fruit tree in the garden is another good place to look for wildlife. Insects live on the trunk, feed on the leaves and on the fruit. The insects in turn attract birds. When the ripe fruit falls to the ground, birds, insects and other creatures come to feed on it.

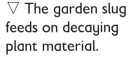
△ The slow-worm often hibernates in a compost heap. The slow-worm is really a legless lizard.

△ The coral spot fungus grows on dead twigs. Millipedes *(below)* and woodlice feed on decaying leaves in the compost heap.

▽ The garden slug feeds on decaying plant material.

The red admiral butterfly *(below)* is very fond of sweet, ripe fruit. When fruit is over-ripe it starts to ferment, producing alcohol. The butterfly sometimes eats so much fermented fruit that it becomes drunk! It cannot fly properly until the effects of the alcohol wears off.

In spring, honey bees *(bottom)* and other insects visit the blossom on fruit trees to feed on the nectar. By doing this, they help to spread the pollen from one tree to the next, which allows the fruit to develop.

The green woodpecker *(bottom right)* likes to feed on ants, which often climb the trunks of fruit trees in search of aphids *(middle right)*. The aphids produce a sweet honeydew which ants feed on.

△ The mistle thrush, which likes mistletoe berries, often nests in fruit trees.

You can look for wildlife in your house at any time of the day or night – you are bound to find something of interest. Remember that most of the animals you see indoors will be temporary visitors from outside, and that your house guests will change with the seasons and the climate.

Many of the wild flowers found in gardens also grow on wastelands and in town parks.

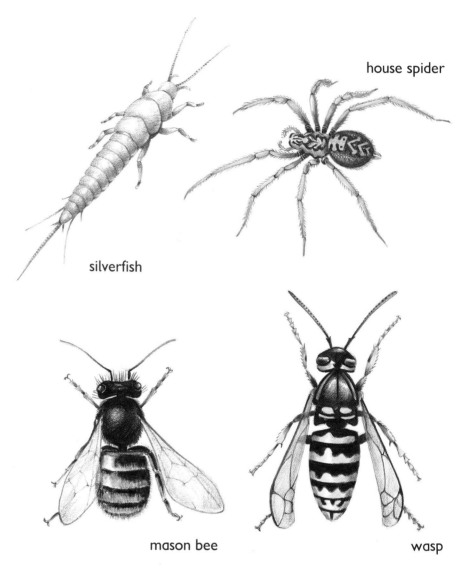

house spider

silverfish

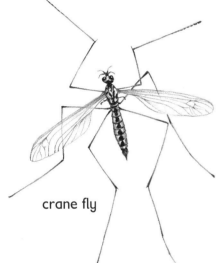

crane fly

mason bee

wasp

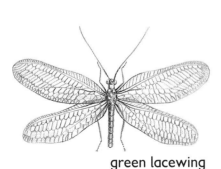

green lacewing

large white butterfly

small tortoiseshell butterfly

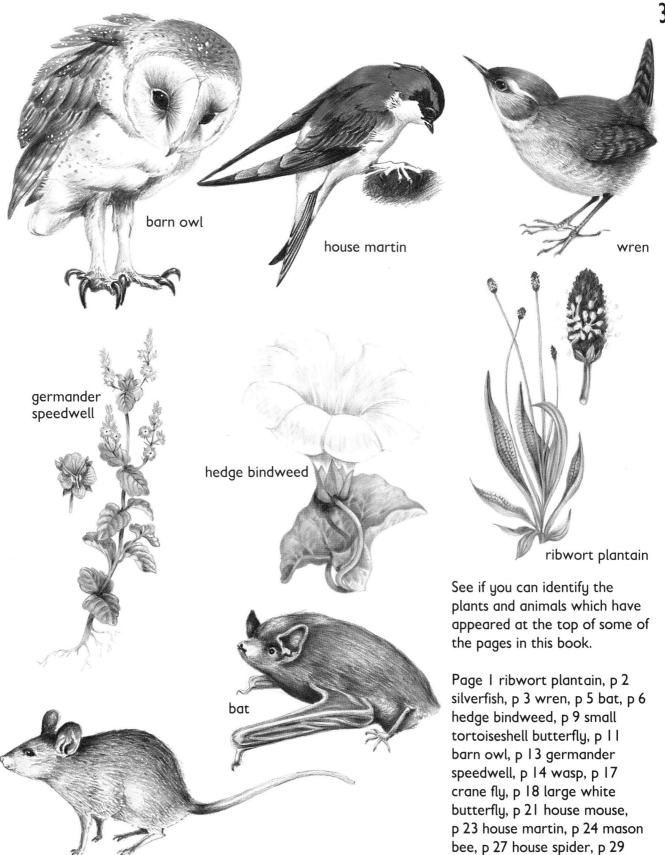

barn owl

house martin

wren

germander speedwell

hedge bindweed

ribwort plantain

bat

house mouse

See if you can identify the plants and animals which have appeared at the top of some of the pages in this book.

Page 1 ribwort plantain, p 2 silverfish, p 3 wren, p 5 bat, p 6 hedge bindweed, p 9 small tortoiseshell butterfly, p 11 barn owl, p 13 germander speedwell, p 14 wasp, p 17 crane fly, p 18 large white butterfly, p 21 house mouse, p 23 house martin, p 24 mason bee, p 27 house spider, p 29 green lacewing